Natural Born Killer

Albert del Toral

iUniverse, Inc.
New York   Bloomington

Natural Born Kidder

iUniverse books may be ordered through booksellers or by contacting:

iUniverse
1663 Liberty Drive
Bloomington, IN 47403
www.iuniverse.com
1-800-Authors (1-800-288-4677)

ISBN: 978-1-4401-1892-0 (pbk)
ISBN: 978-1-4401-1893-7 (ebk)

Printed in the United States of America

iUniverse rev. date: 01/19/2009

Adolf the Red-Neck Reindeer

You know Harvey and Bill Bob,
Bocephus and Bubba,
And Hank and Clebus,
Jebediah, Big Bertha.
But do you recall,
The most famous reindeer of all?

Adolf the red-neck reindeer, (reindeer)
Had a very funny neck, (like a giraffe)
And if you ever saw it, (saw it)
You might even scream "oh, heck!" (like a redneck)
All of the other reindeer (reindeer)
Used to laugh and call him Earl, (like Jason Lee)
They never let poor Adolf, (Adolf)
Laugh along with Minnie Pearl, (what a dumbass!)

Then one drunken Christmas Eve,
Santa came to say, (YEE-HAW!!)
Adolf with your neck strung tight,
Won't you drive my NASCAR right?
Then all the reindeer loved him, (loved him)
And they belched out their praise, (eww, gross!)
"Adolf the red-neck reindeer, (reindeer)
You've dumbed down your very race!" (like George Dubbya)

A Reading From the Book of Victor

I thought I saw an old friend,
While on the scene tonight,
But I quickly came to realize,
He never came into my sight,
I probably just imagined him,
Tonight marks the second year,
And so I'm having a hard time,
Seeing through my every tear.

Buddy, if you hear me,
Let me share the cold-hard truth,
I never really thought,
I'd lose you in our youth,
But ever since I did,
It's aged me quite a bit,
I no longer roam the Earth,
Just a useless little shit.

Remember how each night,
We'd share buckets at the tavern,
How all the waiters knew us,
As if it was our secret cavern,
And if we couldn't pay the tab,
How they'd let us off the hook,
Since they knew we'd be back,
To pay back every cent we took.

Well the last time we did that,
You never did return,
'Cause that stupid motorcycle,
Took my best friend out of turn,
But don't you worry, buddy,
I paid them every cent they earned,
And I also bought a round,
For all our friends who yearned.

It's hard to know I was with you,
That night before your death,

'Cause just a few hours later,
You were living without breath,
And had I still been next to you,
Would I be gone now, too?
And if so, who would repair,
The hearts we broke in two?

Before you left this world behind,
I never knew this cerebral gem,
The living that we do while here,
Is really mostly just for them,
'Cause if I were to go tomorrow,
I wouldn't care nor have a clue,
I'm fine with how I've lived my life,
But my folks would still be blue.

Comforting your mother,
As the tears ran down her face,
Trying to keep your brother,
From going postal at your place,
Helping your dad find meaning,
In a world without his son,
In the most basic of terms,
Were the hardest things I've done.

And though you won't be here,
When I walk down marriage aisle,
Or after my mom passes,
To help resuscitate my smile,
Or to godfather my children,
Weaving yourself into their style,
Still I'm better for having known you,
You made my life worthwhile.

The Slavin'

Once upon a midnight dreary, with my eyes all red and bleary,
For gamma from my monitor had left them tired, confused and sore.
As I sat there crudely hacking, suddenly my lips were smacking,
It was food that I was lacking. My stomach rumbled in my core.
I went to feed, I went to find, perhaps at least an apple core.
- My stomach, I could not ignore.

I soon returned with my cuisine; I brought some coke, for the caffeine,
Also a sandwich, nothing fancy, just some tuna (Albacore).
My assignment nearly ending, to my Prof. I must be sending,
For my grade did need some mending, if my average would be four.
To keep my scholarship in tact, my G.P.A. must be a four.
- This paper, I could not ignore.

When finally done, I went to print, of what would come I had no hint,
When suddenly my coke did spill, upon the keyboard and the floor.
The sad machine gave off a spark, the once-bright screen went briefly dark,
And then my prospects did seem stark. Who else has luck that is so poor?
My lines were gone and in return? An error message, grammar poor.
- Error: **Abort? Retry? Ignore?**

So "R" I pressed with desperate haste, so hours of work I would not waste.
My masterpiece had been written on West Indian herbal lore.
A year ago my paper started, in Pakistan I was imparted,
With a potion that had thwarted, the spreading of a fungal sore.
"Just print!" I prayed so I might publish a new cure for painful sores.
- Error: **Abort? Retry? Ignore?**

"I" I pressed with trepidation. To me, "abort" has connotations.
If the machine had no objections, I'd be willing to ignore,
This annoying interruption. "Come on, desktop, show some gumption,
Let my file avoid corruption; rewriting would be such a chore!"
What was worse, still I did not think that I had time for such a chore.
- Error: **Abort? Retry? Ignore?**

I pressed the "A" feeling quite glum, I could have used a case of rum.
Perhaps while drunk, I would not see my computer's cruel encore.
"Oh dear computer, please be kind." I asked it nice to print my lines,
That some solution it might find, this damn machine whom I deplore.
And then it flickered and I thought, "Was this the option to explore?"
- Error: **Abort**? **Retry**? **Ignore**?

And then my fury came right out, it made me scream and rail about,
The malice and the cruelty of a P.C. that would work no more.
Then with a hammer I did smash, my foul computer which had crashed.
"You always were a piece of trash!" I told the pieces on the floor.
"What have you to say to that?" I asked the screen upon the floor.
- Error: **Abort**? **Retry**? **Ignore**?

Thus was the tale of my worst plight. There never was a hope in sight,
That my paper's wisdom and prose could, to its glory, be restored.
From my school I soon departed, and now I feel most broken hearted,
My degree was truly thwarted, so now I run a liquor store,
Yet in my nightmares I still see that curse which brought me to this store.
- Error: **Abort**? **Retry**? **Ignore**?

The Black Holy

Adorned in silver and black,
They step onto the field,
Like a tribe of pirates sent,
To make the Chargers yield,
Or a group of hunters gathered,
To shoot the Broncos down,
Or a bunch of pillaging maniacs,
Meant to make the Chiefs frown.

And their fans are just as nuts,
With shoulder pads of metal spikes,
Our faces painted so intently,
To scare invasive look-alikes,
And the jerseys on our backs,
Of Bo, Allen, Long and Shell,
Remind every single doubter,
They're about to go through hell.

And now we've got McFadden,
Who might be the missing link,
To complement JaMarcus,
And take us to the brink,
It's now been six long years,
Since we made a playoff run,
But with the pieces now in place,
This here season can be won.

We've accumulated many miles,
Traveling from L.A. to Oak Town,
But now we've settled there again,
And it's time to put our flag down,
So y'all black and yellow bastards,
Does your Pittsburgh still got guts,
Y'know, this ain't the '70s no longer,
If you come, we'll kick your butts.

We've got many fans across the world,
From James Hetfield to George Lopez,
And though your fans are world renown,
When in McAfee, they're all hopeless,
And you can bring the Seahawks, too,
The ones we scared out of the conference,
Hell, we'll take on both of y'all together,
Since our team has so much confidence.

I mean, c'mon, just look around,
A man with two swords through his hat,
That's our freakin' logo, dude,
What do you think of that?
I think it shows we'll bloody murder,
If that's what we must do,
En route to our fourth championship,
There ain't a team we won't subdue.

King of Hell

A leader in my mind,
I live inside my head,
When shit has me down,
It always goes unsaid,
For I can't show emotion,
That might get me mocked,
I'm fighting off insanity,
My brain can't be unlocked.

There're many people like me,
Who live their life on edge,
Being fed their medication,
To keep them off the ledge,
And if they don't take them,
They might become unglued,
Just about anything's possible,
When your reality's askewed.

The one time I got off them,
It was the weirdest thing,
My world morphed into Hell,
And with Satan, I'd a fling,
When he tried controlling me,
I strapped a bomb onto his chest,
Until I chose to trip the wires,
And lay his demon ass to rest.

This is the kind of stuff,
That plays out in my mind,
Axons clash with dendrites,
To leave me quite maligned,
And that's why I'm like this,
Quite unliked by everyone,
Not everyone can understand,
The ninth circle's favorite son.

So just give me several pills,
Leave me caged inside my head,
For if you don't, then who knows,
What craziness might spread,
Maybe I'd become an octopus,
20,000 leagues under the sea,
Or maybe I'd play Don Juan,
To someone who's as warped as me.

Either way, you all know now,
Where you go upon your death,
And if I'm named the king of Hell,
You can bet your every breath,
The fridge I'll stock with liquor,
And the sluts will be my slaves,
Ozzy Osboune and Metallica,
Will come and rock our caves.

Wouldn't it be wicked awesome,
If the next Satan were your friend,
And if you and him together,
Could make your dreams transcend,
For instance, in my underworld,
You'd meet a classy Hemp Fairy,
And you'd get to shag everyone,
Sunjin Kim to Halle Berry.

But since I'm not opposed to God,
We could gladly squash that beef,
I'd open up free trade with Him,
Maybe we'd surf some holy reef,
And wouldn't it be beautiful,
If those dimensions could unite,
And to think, all I must do,
Is forget to take my pills tonight.

Nation of Degradation

The other day, I received an e-mail at dawn,
Which featured a girl getting literally shat on,
And so, of course, this got me to thinking,
To what depths is the human mind sinking?

Just two days later, I was hard at my work,
When my colleague, whom I consider a jerk,
Launched me another, since he'd time to kill,
It was of an Asian girl getting peed on at will.

Seriously, people, how'd y'all lose your souls?
It isn't normal to view women as toilet bowls,
So if these videos give you some twisted thrill,
You should truly consider paying a therapy bill.

And there was even a sicker one, at one point,
Showing a sorority girl getting raped at gunpoint,
To the sick twisted bastard that sent me the latter,
Have you anything left up in your gray matter?

How would you like it, if that'd been your daughter,
That'd been forced to screw, then led out to slaughter?
I don't think you would, so please show some respect,
And certainly don't ever use that to make you erect.

Now before I go, though I don't intend to start a fuss,
Lets try showing common courtesy to those around us,
Since by doing that, surely our world will grow kinder,
I've come around here to give this friendly reminder.

Room 69

Holed up in this Ramada,
We are without T.V.,
Not that that really matters,
Because we have both you and me,
And three days to be alone,
Meshing faint perfumes with spermicide,
So girl, lets make you smell of me,
Way down there, deep inside.

I like you for your brain,
The things you want to analyze;
I like you for your humor,
Mocking all you don't despise;
I like you for your honesty,
The way you seem to tell no lies;
But I also like you for your body,
With green eyes and moonlit thighs.

And honey, the idea of you and I,
Seems better than any from my past;
From the second I met you,
Every second's seemed a blast;
Like you once told me,
Your amazing mind, heart and soul,
Gives me something to be thankful for,
'Cause I guess I like it when we grow.

Now lets make the best of these three days,
Because we haven't us much time;
Lets put an ending to this verse,
By mixing sex into this rhyme;
While you unstrap your bra,
I'll drop my pants unto the floor,
And then we'll hump like bunnies,
'Til the noise starts bugging those next door.

Tick-Tock, Goes the Clock

Back when I was a child,
Having Marvel card exchanges,
I never imagined 20 years,
Would bring about such changes.

Really, it wasn't that long ago,
That it'd be kind of rare to find,
Someone using a computer,
To host their daily grind.

And if you could find someone,
They'd likely be on D.O.S.,
'Cause the Internet was unknown,
By each and every boss.

People's cell phones sat in cars,
Attached by a thick annoying cord,
But without that dang attachment,
Every conversation would be floored.

We watched movies on tapes,
On our old V.C.R. players,
Which at times, when ejected,
Would get stuck within the layers.

And since our T.V. was so ancient,
When you turned off that machine,
The last thing that you watched,
Would stay imprinted on the screen.

Some people possessed beepers,
Which turned us all to nerds,
Since we'd be relaying numbers,
To signify our words.

Unlike the vending machines,
That we boast 'round here today,
Ours couldn't fill prescriptions,
Or feed you condoms out its tray.

And back when I was a child,
Despite my vivid imagination,
I never thought that cloning,
Would be an actual occupation.

Of course, I watched *The Jetsons*,
Each week amongst my friends,
As we all dreamed about flying,
Some futuristic Mercedes-Benz.

And now, here we sit,
Some twenty years later,
Reviewing the blue prints,
Of a car that much greater.

And recently, through evolution,
We learned two things strange,
A team of scientists deduced,
How they thought we would change.

It appears our descendants,
If it is true what was said,
Will have four-fingered hands,
But no natural blond on their head.

Notice how things change,
Far more than we think,
Heck, just the other day,
A robot poured my drink.

Whereas back in the day,
I thought that'd never be,
About twenty years later,
It was happening to me.

To the children among us,
The world housing your lives,
Will likely seem like a relic,
When your future arrives.

Lets hope the changes are good,
So y'all can live without strife,
But it's unknown what awaits,
So please hold on for dear life.

United States of ALmerica

I'm a Hispanic by the name of Alby,
And I need y'all losers to vote for me,
'Cause I wanna fix up your country,
Now that Bush has outlived his infamy.

I'd legalize marriage of the same sex,
Only in California and Massachusetts,
But nowhere else after that law sets,
So relocate where you'll have the best bets.

As for all you anti-war groups,
I'll be recalling all the troops,
And throwing them a party to recoup,
With live music and a game of hoops.

And don't worry about the economy,
I took care of that with mon ami,
Bill Gates paid every last owed penny,
And I've banned the leeching plenty.

Now listen up and believe what you read,
Anybody that can prove a medical need,
See a pharmacist and ask for some weed,
But I'm taxing that to fix our budget, indeed.

Speaking of which, there'll be no new taxes,
Besides the weed one, taxed to those asses,
And some others will be chopped by my axes,
Unnecessary ones will be named in my faxes.

And abortions, since that's an issue of perplexity,
Will only be allowed, when handled responsibly,
Like if you've been raped or it'll hurt extensibly,
Then we'll use tubes to leave your tummy empty.

For everyone else, those therein unmentioned,
You'll just have to opt for the adoption method,
But we'll need to get the old law contentioned,
Before we can let folks do as they're destined.

And as for religion, practice what you want,
That ain't an area the government should haunt,
Just try to practice it in a way nonchalant,
For if you piss people off, their anger may flaunt.

Who I Am

I use booze to socialize,
'Cause my skin's like a disguise.
I use birth control during sex,
'Cause having kids would be a hex.
I eat my veggies so I can live,
Though if I died, nothing would give.
And I work my ass off for the cash,
'Cause I'm just white-collared trash.

To spread their legs, I use my tongue.
To unlock minds, I quote Carl Jung.
To help this world, do charity,
Don't curse them with vulgarity.
I know how to get things done,
Though finding me, I've just begun.
Help me learn just who I am,
Before I turn into the Son of Sam.

When I sleep, I dream a lot,
About the knights in Camelot.
When I paint, I sketch strange things,
Like humans chasing after wings.
When I read, my mind rebels,
It's like these lands live in my cells.
When I write, that's my escape,
What separates me from the ape.

I'll droop my head before I cry,
And hide the truth after I lie.
I'll lock my door once I'm inside,
Though it's been open since you died.
I tell jokes to break the tension,
And I only work thanks to a pension.
I've got tattoos that make me pretty,
To hide my mind when not so witty.

But still I've got no one to love,
Save those few that fled above.
I do not know what I've done wrong,
Tired of singing the same old song.
The many stories that I tell,
Are birthed within my empty shell.
A story's nothing without a crowd,
I think my living's not allowed.

Lord, I'm praying, let me be,
Just someone nice eventually.
Earth, I love you, yes I do,
From Niger to Kalamazoo.
Hey music, man, thanks again,
You're the one keeping me zen.
And to all the rest of y'all,
Please don't ever drop the ball.

I use words to frame ideas,
While my mouth drains pizzerias.
I use feelings to get my way,
In the manipulative U.S.A.
I bury thoughts in your ashtray,
Knowing you'll toss that ash away.
No matter who is loved on Earth,
We die alone, so what's it worth?

To spread their ash, means they have soared.
To spread their ass, means they have whored.
To help this world, don't be it's slave,
Be something more, be someone brave.
See, I know how to get things done,
Though finding me, I've just begun.
Help me learn just who I am,
Don't let me be some useless sham.

Unhappily Ever After

I dreamt I was a song note,
Amused by all my fears,
And on my song, I tread along,
Just guiding you through years.
Doesn't everything seem better,
When you know that I am here?
No matter what the problem be,
My solution's very clear.

I dreamt I had a brain once,
Which often saw no light,
And when the switch would flip on,
That'd only start a fight,
Then one day, a shmoe decided,
It's wiring was too tight,
He played with it, the loosening,
Made everything seem right.

Now I'm sitting here alone,
Not knowing what to do,
I'm so used to shit effing up,
When it's right, I've got no clue,
Maybe I'm experiencing the nirvana,
That only an elite few ever see,
But I kinda miss the agony,
That comes with missing ecstacy.

I dreamt I spoke to God one night,
While he smoked up on my lawn,
And though that sounds quite blasphemous,
I can't control things inter-yawn,
God took a toke, then looked at me,
He said, "listen up, my son,
The answer's up in Heaven,
And some day, on you, it'll dawn."

I dreamt that later on that night,
Some gremlin ate my face,
And though I tried to fight him off,
I couldn't keep his pace,
He had a genie there beside him,
Who was a mental case,
He wished away my happiness,
As he dressed himself in lace.

Now I'm sitting here all glum,
And it makes me feel so great,
I'm used to things not working out,
So this right here's my fate,
Having stumbled toward utopia,
I smelled the putrid scent of hate,
But now things smell so rosy,
Since I heard her say "I'm late."

SPACEctomy

If we traveled to space, I'd hide from you,
I'd lay in a crater, somewhere out of view,
I'd sit there thinking, how you've done me wrong,
And I'd come up with lyrics, create my own song.

If we traveled together, somewhere like the moon,
Chartering new territory, during our honeymoon,
I'd leave you at the base, to climb up to the top,
From which I would jump, to Earth I would drop.

If we went to Saturn, to slip and slide on the rings,
To put up with you, I'd need to bring a few things,
Duct tape for your mouth, and rope for each hand,
The more I contain you, the less you'll demand.

If we went to Mars, where we discovered new life,
I'd get me some space money, by trading you, wife,
Then I'd help the green folks, strap you to their chair,
And as they anal probed you, I'd just laugh and stare.

If we could roam space, on our own shooting star,
We'd be traveling quicker, than in any sports car,
Lets race one another, like way back in our youth,
And once I outrun you, I'll bust out my vermouth.

If you wanted to kiss, amidst the stars in Draco,
I'd be like Richard Ramirez, that one day in Waco,
Put a hole in your head, until the wind starts to whistle,
Maybe take it a step further, strap you to a missile.

If we were the only souls, floating the Milky Way,
I'd find a black hole, and float you that way,
And once you got sucked in, I'd get away fast,
Each year after that, that holiday'd be a blast.

Ape Rape, or: How I Learned to Stop Running and Love the Yeti

One day, in the Pacific Northwest,
I saw this thing quite unlike the rest,
Which stood taller than Robert Wadlow,
But was covered in hair from head to toe.
Holy crap, man, don't you get me?
I think that I saw a freakin' Yeti!

So anyway, there I was out in the woods,
Taking a piss, so I was gripping the goods,
When suddenly, I heard noises behind me,
And I turned around, to meet a horny Yeti,
This obscure creature hadn't had sex in a year,
Which I guess would turn any ape-man queer.

But see, here's the problem I saw,
I didn't want that thing's flesh in my jaw,
Because unlike him, I've not had a dry spell,
And that thing was huge, so I let out a yell,
Then I ran away, quicker than the Flash,
Wouldn't take that foot-long, for no amount of cash.

But this Yeti was in heat, so he gave chase,
I had no choice, so I busted out the mace,
When he got close, I sprayed his eyes,
That just turned him on, much to my surprise,
So he reached forward, shoved me in a ditch,
And before I knew it, he'd made me his bitch.

And now that I've finally got away,
I'm needing therapy like every day,
So if ever you come across a giant ape,
That seems to have a man-like shape.
Holy hell, man, don't you stop to see,
Just run like hell, for it may be horny!

Friday Night

I'm throwing a bonfire,
To have fun with the gang,
So starting at six-ish,
Come for beer and poontang.

What's my excuse for the fire?
A buddy just got to town;
So I'm inviting everybody,
Who's down to get down.

Don't anybody start a fight,
Cave only to the sublime,
'Cause tonight's Friday night,
We all just want a good time.

If we all work together,
Then stories'll be made,
'Cause we'll surely get drunk,
And we might even get laid.

Love My Soldiers

Though I may protest a war or two,
I'd never protest the likes of you,
Since this great freedom that we claim,
Came to us signed in your great name.

Thank you, soldiers of the U.S.A.,
For giving up your every day,
To better the world America knows,
By protecting us from distant foes.

And to all my friends now overseas,
Return home safe, I ask you please,
From ex-girlfriends to a close friend,
I'll see you all, upon war's end.

When y'all return to these great states,
I'll pick y'all up at airport gates,
And we'll go party like nothing's changed,
I won't let time leave y'all shortchanged.

It's all I can do for all you've risked,
For packing up and being whisked,
To a place where you're fresh meat,
Since landmines wait on triggering feet.

And I can't envision your entire story,
Since the films we see are far less gory,
With y'all getting shot at 'round the clock,
Maybe some of your friends fell to the glock.

But for risking limbs and standing proud,
To secure these freedoms we're allowed,
I know your job ain't an easy one,
So thanks again for all you've done.

The Vixen Dubbed "Conviction"

Oh sweet Gina Carano,
I hope the bad news ain't true,
But if you're now unemployed,
Then my heart beats for you.

So Xtreme Combat's no more,
Since Kimbo lost in fourteen,
Which leaves you a free agent,
Although a big part of that scene.

If it makes you feel better,
Though the title shot's gone,
You're still an *American Gladiator*,
Who's getting her video game on.

And if the U.F.C. doesn't bite,
Meaning it rejects each femme,
Don't you worry, darling,
'Cause you don't need them.

What you need is a man,
Who's, like, five-eleven,
Weighs about a buck seventy,
And is good with the pen.

Maybe a Spanish last name,
And a background in fights,
So you'll have stuff in common,
When you turn out the lights.

Y'all should wrestle in bed,
'Cause I'm sure he won't mind,
In fact, he can't even fathom,
Of a better way to unwind.

And this man that I speak of,
His face can't be clearer,
In fact, I saw him today,
Trapped inside my mirror.

So sweet Gina Carano,
Won't you let me mix in?
I know you're a bad-ass,
But can you be my vixen?

What Ever Happened to Brittany Murphy?

Girl, when I saw you in *Clueless*,
You looked like a geek,
But when I saw you the next time,
You'd become this beautiful freak,
You went from a *Girl, Interrupted*,
To topping my *Little Black Book*,
And suddenly I'd walk me *8 Mile*,
To get a much closer look.

While I was *Riding in Cars with Boys*,
And discussing every *Summer Catch*,
You were out filming *Just Married*,
In which you acted like you were into Asht,
But in my dreams there was no Mr. Kutcher,
Just you and I living alone in *Sin City*,
You being a total *Uptown Girl*,
And me being extra smitty.

But then something strange happened,
You grew some *Happy Feet*,
And walked away from Hollywood,
Leaving me there with that defeat,
I haven't seen someone so *Drop Dead Gorgeous*,
Since the year 2005,
Would it kill you to come check in with me,
And let me know you're still alive?

Say Uncle

Turns out, my sister's pregnant,
Her kid will soon have much to learn,
But when she announced her intent,
All I could think about was her sojourn.

I'd forgotten how speedy our lives go,
Seems like just yesterday, her and I,
Were sitting around the Nintendo,
Waiting for the other's player to die.

But now, she'll give birth soon,
To a little baby girl or boy,
So come about the end of June,
I'll be blessed with an uncle's joy.

And really, what do I know,
About raising such a little thing,
Not much, but I hope I can learn,
For this is really happening.

And I'm one of only a select few,
Responsible for raising mini-her,
But I've still gotta raise me, too,
So how I'll do that, I am still unsure.

I'm hoping we won't screw it up,
Since none of us knows what to do,
I'm guessing we'll find out what's up,
The minute we go clean it's poo.

To be honest, I think this baby,
Will meet an awesome fate,
For my sister is a decent lady,
And my bro-in-law is great.

Here comes the next chapter in our story,
Which I expect will change us a lot,
Hopefully the baby'll learn things from me,
Or better yet, maybe not.

Step Two

It's Friday night,
And my tired ass is home,
Typing this shit,
Relaxing my dome,
Sitting in my backyard,
Enjoying the breeze,
Savoring a cold one,
With laptop on knees.

My headphoned ears,
Plugged into the P.C.,
Have me enjoying iTunes,
Ludwig's ninth symphony,
It's quite the lovely night,
But I'm glad no one's here,
'Cause in just four days,
I'll be aging one more year.

And it's nice to have a break,
From the real world I know,
'Cause to me it seems,
I've never had time to grow,
There's always something,
Always some kind of drama,
Sirened ambulance in the park,
Constant nagging from mama.

I just need some alone time,
Time to catch up with my brain,
Figure out what I want from life,
What things I should try to attain,
I need to get on some path now,
For 25 ain't that young anymore,
I'm too old to depend on my folks,
But too young to become a bore.

Luckily, I've already got a good job,
That was step one and it's done,
Now comes step number two,
To try and find my true "one,"
If such a person exists for me,
She'd need to have it together,
And since I'm an admitted fuck-up,
She'd need to make me look better.

Considering whom I've already dated,
I don't need another wild one,
Just someone who understands me,
And gets that I ain't ready to have a son,
I just need a loyal partner in crime,
Someone with whom to share a joke,
I ain't as picky as some people say,
I don't even care if they drink or smoke.

So long as this person makes me happy,
That's all I'm really looking for here,
Even if that makes me sound needy,
Still I feel I need to make that clear,
For I've had my heart broken before,
And honestly that does not feel fun,
So this time I'm seeking a decent gal,
Who will look out for me in the long run.

Step two seems simple enough on paper,
But trust me, it's hard as hell to apply,
So I'm hoping I find success out in the field,
I really hope things don't again go awry,
'Cause if all goes according to plan,
Then maybe soon I'll be a step three candidate,
"But what's step three," you ask?
To know my life can be whatever I make of it.

Freak Magnet

I must have a chip implanted,
Deep inside my brain,
That attracts a kind of woman,
So pretty, yet insane.
The kind that wants kids,
At only 18 years of age.
The kind that, ten years later,
Still lives on minimum wage.
The kind that nearly O.D.s,
Just to excite her every day.
The kind that gets drunk,
So that she can claim to be gay.
The kind that drives crunked,
Then does some stupid shit,
That starts beef with a cop,
Which she'll later try to hit.
The kind that grabs a razor,
And goes slicing up a vein.
The kind that gets happy,
When the weather turns to rain.
The kind that wants marriage,
After only date two;
And when I say no,
She claims I must be gay, too.
The kind that joins the army,
The day we enter into war;
Is then sent away to fight,
But bitches 'bout the gore.
What about these weirdos,
Even turns me on at first?
Why do I think they're cool,
Until their true intentions burst?

A : S :: D : V

This gal has tattooed wrists,
With four letters clearly seen,
But they all drive me nuts,
Since I know not what they mean.

On one wrist it says "D.V.,"
And the other reads "A.S."
So I made "Darth Vader,"
And "Anakin," my guess.

Then I figured something else,
"A" for "Abuelo," "D" for "Dad;"
Might she possibly be remembering,
The two strongest men she had?

But then it struck me silly,
Like a punch straight to the chest,
What if those letters repped a gang,
Maybe my ignorance was best?

I do not know the answer,
For when I asked, she got all cryptic,
Which makes me kind of wonder,
Has she some truth apocalyptic?

Church of Sexual Transmission

Oh man, I'm burning,
So tell me what's this…
A green color I'm turning,
You gave me Syphilis!

Oh man, my thigh,
Is starting to twitch…
These skin folds don't lie,
You gave me jock itch!

Oh man, my liver,
It feels so inflamed…
With Hep. B, I shiver,
I feel so ashamed!

Oh man, my skin,
With superficial burrows…
You brought scabies so thin,
To our sex intramurals.

Oh man, my eyes,
I'm losing my sight…
Your oral surprise,
Gave me trachoma tonight!

Oh man, my life,
You done messed it up…
Thanks to you, wife,
I'm a dirty old schlup!

Trumped

Let me share a story,
That happened years ago,
When I was still a waiter,
With nowhere I could go.

I ran into a fellow,
Sucking on his thumb,
So what the heck's the matter,
Seems he'd had too much rum.

I dragged him to the back,
Where I laid him on the floor,
I took his fatty wallet,
And I locked that cooler door.

That dude was carrying money,
So much, I soon learned why,
When I read his license,
Donald Trump was that there guy.

So I quit and ran away,
As quickly as I could,
Because I knew just sitting there,
Would surely do no good.

I bought myself a jet plane,
And I flew across the sea,
I doctored up a new face,
And had plastic surgery.

I even changed my name,
From "Al" to "Sergio,"
And never did I contact,
Anyone I used to know.

With the Donald's money,
I bought some happiness,
Two lovely Swedish hookers,
Whom I quickly did undress.

I purchased me a Tesla,
The rarest of its kind,
Then I bought myself a mansion,
Where I could go unwind.

This was the life I led,
For many months and years,
A pool so full of models,
A fridge so full of beers.

Until that fateful day,
The truth all came to light,
And the minute that it did,
My riches went goodnight.

Donald showed up at my door,
A bodyguard there by his side,
So I tried to get away,
But still they beat my ass with pride.

His guard punched me with brass knucks,
Trump broke a bottle on my head,
And thank God that I'm so tough,
Or else I'd probably now be dead.

So if you ever spot that richie,
Send him my regards,
And tell him I am suing him,
And all his freakin' guards!

Heartless

I woke up this morning, feeling out of whack,
Since I'd had a dream, that a heart I did lack,
And what's worse, I put my hand to my chest,
But I hadn't a pulse, from what I could digest,
So I got dressed up, and I headed out the door,
To the doctor's office, to take scans of my core,
And what came back was something very odd,
There was no heart found inside my bod!

So the two of us, just my doctor and I,
Wondered out loud how I'd gone awry,
And to where my heart had disappeared,
And how my survival without it was weird,
But putting all scientific facts aside,
To find my heart, we tried and tried,
We pulled my pockets out, one by one,
And then we looked outside, under the great big sun.

Wherever we looked, only failed results turned up,
It wasn't in any of my drawers, nor in my favorite cup,
We even x-rayed my snake, but it wasn't in him,
So I changed clothes, and headed toward the gym,
It hadn't plopped off any of the treadmills,
Nor had it been discovered in anyone's pills,
As I started to wonder if I'd ever get back my heart,
I was suddenly taken all the way back to the start.

I sprung up in bed, smashed my head on the lamp,
And I thought to myself, as my leg started to cramp,
Of course it was a dream, since nothing else made sense,
But why has each dream gotten more and more intense,
And as I pondered this to myself, my mind reminisced,
About a really sexy dream in which Keira and I'd kissed,
So suddenly, my dreams didn't seem so dang bad,
And I rolled out of bed, like the world's jolliest lad.

Deadtime Story

I need to talk this through,
But I'm not all that sure with who,
My eyes have framed an image,
Of this lady, five-foot-two,
She's sitting on a rocking chair,
And I, the toddler, lay weezing in my crib,
The night is cold, the lights are off,
A story's slipping through her lips,
But before I'm taught the moral,
In my world of no disorder,
My light brown eyes fell asleep,
And they woke up out of order,
'Cause now all that has changed,
And I'm pondering life's meaning,
When grandma flew away,
My mind really got to cleaning,
If no one really ever dies,
Like that cruel doctor joked,
She might still pop out that coffin,
Since she never really croaked,
And we'll laugh aloud,
I think that's what I dreamt about,
While she read out loud,
Though its truth, I doubt,
Hard to expect a wish that old,
To be true in my present shame,
But either way, as I have told,
I'll never be the same!

Voice

As long as I'm alive,
I'll have a voice,
And as long as I do,
Using it ain't a choice,
There're wrongs to right,
And folks who can't,
So I'm here for them,
My voice won't recant.

No one should get abused,
For the color of their skin,
We should look inside,
And cherish what's within,
No one should be preyed upon,
Because they pray alone,
Let them be who they are,
Don't put hate on a throne.

Pick-Up Game

Went to the pool hall, just the other day,
Flirted with a brunette, who'd been looking my way,
I bought her a drink, as I wielded my lumber,
She liked how I think, so she gave me her number,
Bored a few days later, I gave her a call,
I said, "Hey, it's Albert, we met at the hall,"
We spoke up a storm, then we made us a date,
And we had us some fun, 'til that day became late.

Epitaph

Herein lies Albert del Toral,
Who died really piss-ass drunk,
Since he never could live down,
That one girl puking on his junk.

But really, it's for the better,
That jerk always drank our beer,
So lets go dig him up right now,
And shove some cans into his rear.

Spare Me Your Change

I am that boy, with a genius mind,
That has a problem, I drink to unwind,
And I won't listen to you, so don't give me advice,
While I'm pouring my Scotch, onto cubes of ice.

I've tried dating girls, but it never works out,
'Cause when things get good, I tend to blackout,
And they have no clue, of what they should think,
I don't love them more, than I loved my last drink.

I am that guy, who shows up at work,
Acting all silly, since I've drunk like a jerk,
The whole night before, was spent at the bars,
Roaming about, just drowning my scars.

It's not that I've gone, and given up on this life,
I just like the taste, that distracts from my strife,
And if that's a problem, that's all right with me,
Just pass me a bottle, and hide my car key.

The happiness I've known, has all been an illusion,
Some people call it a problem, but it's my solution,
And we all have a vice, so I really ain't strange,
So next time we meet, please spare me your change.

Gay Poem

It's been said many times before,
That I carry myself like a whore,
And in living my life as such,
I've been rather open to much,
But lately I've realized something,
I may be the last twenty-something,
Who hasn't tried the gay lifestyle,
Nor have I even perused that aisle.

See, the thing with that is this,
I've no desire to feel a man's kiss,
That's not to say I'm opposed to that,
So don't start that gossipy chat,
'Cause I'm one hundred percent for it,
I believe that lifestyle can be real legit,
But only to those who really are gay,
Not just followers of the trend today.

And yes, it's definitely a trend today,
Since half the queers ain't really gay,
Most of them just do it for show,
Like that fire-crotch known as "LiLo,"
Maybe Angelina Jolie before her,
Or Madonna, the style's entrepreneur,
And Anne Heche, most notoriously,
All who faked it so laboriously.

With many people really being that way,
Why do attention whores like to play,
Leave being gay to those who were achin',
People like Lance Bass or *Idol*'s Clay Aiken,
My girls Ellen Degeneres and Portia de Rossi,
The Smith's lead singer, Steven Morrissey,
And, of course, hilarious Neil Patrick Harris,
Not pretentious fools like that wannabe Paris.

When you're faking it, it isn't hard to see,
Just look at t.A.T.u, if you don't believe me,
So why not step back and stay out the way,
Of what Rosie and Elton are doing today,
Because I know that there's no way in hell,
That it's true the story that all these stats tell,
Right now, half my friends claim they're gay,
And one in ten people claim swinging that way.

And though I support granting gay rights,
Legalizing marriage and fighting good fights,
There's no way in hell, that I can support,
People who lie, causing the movement to thwart,
All of these jerks are hurting these folk,
By turning their struggles into a joke,
And if this continues, no straights will remain,
Just try to tell me that that's not insane?

So in closing, I'd just like to request,
Leave being gay to those who were blessed,
And if you're straight, then lying's bizarre,
Be proud to be you, since that's what you are,
There's no shame in being part of the crowd,
Such shame only lies in not standing proud,
And trust me when I say, that it is all right,
Straight people can still help gays in their plight.

Wise Man

Since a cold winter fog crept,
The gates were shut, and so,
We weren't allowed to board,
Our plane in Heathrow.

As I stared out the window,
Just taking in the white snow,
I heard the guy next to me,
Speak these words so low.

He said, "Boy, what's the matter?
You look like you've been let down.
Did you have Christmas plans,
Or do you just like to frown?"

So I took off my mittens,
And I stared back at my judge,
I asked if he'd ever felt,
That fate held a grudge?

He took some sips of coffee,
Until the words he could find,
He swore fate results from,
Our own subconscious mind.

He said luck's nonexistent,
Everything happens for a reason,
So if I felt like wallowing,
This ain't the correct season.

So I'm stuck in a snow storm,
By myself, here in London?
Things could be much worse,
I could be dying in a dungeon.

And then came the kicker,
That's where he had been,
Just a year before this stranding,
He was living life in sin.

Back in his native Kansas,
He'd had an affair with crank,
Shoving needles in his arm,
One day he walked Death's plank.

He still doesn't know how,
He survived that last Christmas,
But he's thankful to be stranded,
Now, with the snow and us.

And this made me aware that,
My situation was far from the worst,
What with folks starving everywhere,
And the orphans who've been cursed.

Many people on our planet,
Face a much harder lifestyle,
For they haven't any money,
And they've had none in a while.

There're folks who've lost close ones,
Around this time of year,
And so when the season returns,
They can't help but shed a tear.

He said, "Kids with mental illness,
Live unaware of their own being,
So if snow's your biggest problem,
Then may I suggest you go skiing?"

"See, Christmas is a time to smile,
Being thankful for the gift of life,
So if you're gonna act the Grinch,
I think it's time you learn real strife."

The man beside me's smart,
His message was insightful,
He took my silly outlook,
And made me much less spiteful.

Who cares, so I missed Christmas,
What's one night in a lifetime?
Really, I shouldn't complain,
For my life's been so sublime.

Win Her Back

This one chick, I leant my heart to,
She stomped it and she broke it in two,
Now every other gal I do,
Reminds me of the one that made me so blue.

One day, I'll win her back,
But when I do, she'll live on her knees,
Yeah, keep feeding me all your flack,
It gives me more time to figure out a way to kill the one I cannot please.

And while my mind goes to town,
I'm letting yet another one let me down.

Here she comes, the unintelligible whiz,
Who doesn't communicate herself well;
She thinks she knows everything there is,
But she'll know nothing more of me once I send her to hell.

Oh, she really pulls my strings,
Once she pulled so hard, I thought I'd grown some wings.

But there was one I tried with whom it almost did work,
I just don't think my heart was ready for that;
The fact she didn't bother me, really bothered this jerk,
Sure she wasn't perfect, but she was pleasant in chat.

So wait 'til I win the grouch back,
When I bring her bags in, I'll place them on the bed,
And when first she goes to attack,
She'll see my eyes fixed on the one who played nice with my head.

I'm gonna win, all right?
I'm gonna win her back!

Born To Be A Waiter

You were born to be a waiter,
At your favorite restaurant,
There wouldn't be none greater,
At doing what they want.

Take a good look at yourself,
Tell me what else could you be,
You look like a Keebler elf,
Or at least you do to me.

You can't do any math,
And you can't barely read,
But you can sell some meth,
While toked-out on your weed.

So come and be my waiter,
Stop thinking you're too hood,
Just bring me the cheese grater,
And I'll tip you something good.

And I know how this works,
As I was once in your shoes,
You've dated all these jerks,
So whose spit is in my booze?

You were born to be a waiter,
And your tattoos tell that story,
You wouldn't make a good dictator,
So just go take inventory.

I know you know the gossip,
Of every person up in here,
But don't you let nothin' slip,
'Bout the felon nor the queer.

Oh, and please do me a favor,
Bring me some more napkins,
Leaving me here alone to savor,
Shit so unapproved by Atkins.

You were born to be a waiter,
So keep on partying, girly,
And don't take me for a hater,
Or I'll collect your tip-out early.

Boy Without A Family

The boy without a family,
The man who's on his own,
His poppy's out in Bimini,
Mom's always got a bone,
He tries to see his sister,
The club doesn't let him in,
His ear now grows a blister,
The stomach's wearing thin.

The boy without a family,
The man who's on his own,
His friends throughout Miami,
Have left him all alone,
Victims of their weddings,
Some hangin' with a child,
Of all the freakin' endings,
Why choose the one so mild?

The boy without a family,
The man who's on his own,
He knows not any amity,
He has no skills to hone,
He doesn't own a thing,
With pockets short of change,
His eyes now start to sting,
As his mind starts to derange.

The boy without a family,
Now the man that time forgot,
He's barely kept his sanity,
Never getting what he sought,
And soon he'll be too old,
To really even give a crap,
This is the man y'all sold,
To walk into your trap.

I'Merica

I was born dirt poor,
90 miles off your shore,
Right near Club Tropicana,
Inside the town of Havana.

Aside from Varadero Beach,
I don't know what they teach,
But living in Cuba's not fun,
Just ask anyone.

If I could reach out my hand,
To lay a finger upon your land,
And I truly promised to behave,
Would my raft resist each wave?

I just want to raise my clan,
Where I needn't fear the man,
And I want a chance to be happy,
By being more than I'm told to be.

If Old Glory waved on my porch,
And Lady Liberty offered her torch,
I'd be one of the most thankful men,
Ever to be deemed an "American."

Roid Busters

Y'know, I'm getting tired of these guys,
Every day, it's some new surprise,
I get that they want to look strong,
That maybe it helps them belong,
But just 'cause they're on the juice,
They think they can come and abuse,
I mean, look at our gym these days,
It's been torn apart in so many ways,
It's like a troll breaks every machine,
Making that part of his daily routine,
And then there's the cracked glass,
I mean, really, who was the dumbass,
Who came and tossed the dumbbell,
That bounced, and smashed it to hell?

I don't get how people can be so silly,
Well, I don't get many things, really,
Don't think I didn't notice the "no steroid" signs,
Ripped off the walls by some of you swines,
And why are there so many broken locker shelves,
It seems like y'all really love to stare at yourselves,
I've even seen pictures taken – how insane,
I mean, seriously, can you be any more vain?
Why not just post up a poster of you,
Flexing your bicep, maybe getting a clue,
Let others sit there and admire your pump,
As they shove steroid needles into their rump,
And maybe you'll be the next Gregg Valentino,
Hell, I bet that'd be your pipe dream, though!

I'd never agree with what steroids give,
But whatever, your life's your prerogative,
Do what you must, and live on each whim,
But stop yourself short of destroying our gym,
The next time your bullshit comes to my chagrin,
Oh, you'll be the one who takes it on the chin,
I'll call Roid Busters to clean up your mess,
'Cause now my gym houses drugs in excess,

So in they will come with their retro jumpsuits,
With pictures of needles exed out by their roots,
And they'll run tests on every one of you guys,
Then ride off to their labs, where they'll analyze,
And once the results come back, so will they,
To karate chop you freaks and lock y'all away.

Minority President

I'm so proud of my America,
For overcoming its prejudice,
And electing the black candidate,
To complete slavery's exodus.

On November 4th, 2008,
We brought together all the races,
Maybe now my future presidents,
Could even have Hispanic traces.

In the course of just a couple months,
When Barack enters into office,
He'll undo Bush's evil regime,
Though some folks still remain standoffish.

Personally, I think Obama,
As socialist as he may now seem,
Will bring great change to our old nation,
At least that's my "American dream."

For whatever this man does right now,
Affects every non-white resident,
So he better do great things and soon,
Or we'll lose our chance at president.

Please Obama, we're rooting for you,
Prove to these people what we can do,
For I finally feel accepted,
And losing that vibe would make me blue.

You are like a savior to us all,
Giving the minority an equal voice,
So please come true on your promises,
And allow my people to rejoice.

How to Look Stupid and Ruin Your Life

A while ago, my dumb ass got caught,
Selling an enormous amount of pot,
They dressed me in light brown fatigues,
And booked me into the F.D.C.

Then they taught me about electricity,
'Cause that was my job inside that fake city,
Paid forty-two cents an hour 'cause I was lucky,
Unlike most of these folks, I'd a college degree.

I remember counting down my release date,
While serving three months as a federal inmate,
And since my fifth floor unit seemed like a cage,
I'd never even stopped to think about my probation stage.

But being released like that is annoying, too,
Since they monitor just about all you do,
You're on E.M., but need to go somewhere,
You'll call their number, try to make them care.

Then today, it messed with my son the same,
He asked me, "Daddy, you coming to my game?"
I had to dial a number, which told me yes,
I do, in fact, have a code-a-phone test.

So no, my son, I cannot show up,
Today, your daddy pees into a cup,
With some dude watching him do so,
I hope that dude gets to enjoy the show.

What my P.O. doesn't understand,
Is that despite having sold my brand,

That doesn't mean I ever smoked the stuff,
It just means my wallet ain't ever had enough.

So for the next seventy-two months strong,
They'll treat me like I'm Tommy Chong,
And my every action they will now enshrine,
In a green folder with a five-numbered spine.

So hey, welcome to probation, y'all,
This is where you go when from your perch you fall,
So think about this the next time you act the fool,
You can lose your freedom, if you break the rule.

Dream Girl

She has legs like Stacy Keibler,
And a mouth like Ms. Jolie;
She's got dimples like Carano,
Yet she's got the hots for me;
And her eyes, just like Fiona's,
Tell stories with no sound;
While her booty, like Shakira's,
Leaves me very tightly wound.

She's got breasts like Pamela,
On the coldest winter night;
With abs like Keira Knightley's,
So defined they cause delight;
With a brain like Maya Angelou's,
Her words resolve a lot;
Her grace, like Audrey Hepburn's,
Ties your heart into a knot.

When the lights go out at night,
She makes me wonder things unsaid,
Like could such a girl exist,
Somewhere outside my head?
And if such a girl came 'round,
Would I know what words to speak,
Or would my brain lock up my jaw,
Make me seem like some weird freak?

I think my dream's created,
A girl whom every guy would want,
And my vision hates my brain now,
For such an image can't but haunt;
I guess that's why my mind,
Shouldn't ever go amiss,
'Cause how can any girl that's real,
Come even close to matching this?

Once you've met the perfect gal,
If even just within sleep's zone,
There's no other who can replace,
Seems you're doomed to live alone;
Think I've screwed myself forever,
Now every girl will disappoint,
So I'll probably never date again,
'Cause what the hell's the point?

Masturbation Baby

I'm a man, got a hand,
Can't no girl ever rape this land,
If she tries, I've got feet,
And I'll leave in ways not discreet,
See me walk, see me run,
See me grab and shoot off my gun,
In the street, in the air,
I will swim even if I'm bare.
It's masturbation, baby!

Waving fists, drawing near,
Shouting things you don't care to hear,
Talking smack, talking trash,
Did you know beards can cause a rash?
In my head, in my ears,
Keep this up and I'll drown in my beers,
Listen up, silly one,
I'm just a lay, so don't call me "hun."
It's masturbation, baby!

Worship me, love my mind,
Just get away when I try to unwind,
Take a knee, bow to it,
Do what you want 'cause I don't give a shit,
Forget your love, ignore my hate,
I love the fact that you ain't all that great,
Admire me, enjoy the ride,
I'm feeling horny, way down deep inside.
It's masturbation, baby!

You yell at me, I give two shits,
I'll think about it as I smother your tits,
You slap my face, I'll fuck your ass,
I'm sorry, didn't mean to come off as crass,
You tell some lies, you spread some dirt,
So bet your ass that this just might hurt,
But it'll be fun, like some sick dream,
Might just leave you sipping at the cream.
It's masturbation, baby!

Lover's Trance

I got a lady,
All men observe,
She gives me lovin',
That I don't deserve,
I'm staying loyal,
To calm her nerve,
'Cause I am pleased by,
Each wondrous curve.

I'm amazed,
I pulled this off,
A girl so cool,
Who doesn't scoff,
A smoking body,
I once dreamt of,
With jet black hair,
And a cutesy cough.

I think I'm done,
Searching around,
'Cause I have found,
One so profund,
And my love's,
So tightly bound,
We'll tie the knot,
Then she'll be crowned.

I'm amazed,
I've had this chance,
And I'm surprised,
By my romance,
I never thought,
I'd be one to dance,
Through the future,
In a lover's trance.

Slave Labor

My mama's a teacher,
And my dad drives a boat,
So whatever you heard,
Must be some kind of joke,
I ain't ever had cash,
I've been closer to broke,
And that'll be my life,
Until the day that I croak.

I'm not saying life sucks,
I'm just saying it's tough,
Especially for children,
Who have it so rough,
The ones busting their ass,
For a dollar a day,
I'm not one of those,
Still I've something to say.

If you pirate your music,
Or wear name-brand shoes,
If you shop at Wal-Mart,
You should be in the news,
For killing some children,
Those who've suffered abuse,
Bleeding in sweat shops,
Making stuff you can lose.

I've also suffered a bit,
Within my personal life,
But none of my shit,
Competes with such strife,
These kids have it bad,
Carving shit with a knife,
And if they misbehave,
They'll be shot with a rif.

No questions asked,
That's their motto, you see,
"Chank-chank-chank,"
Sounds the screaming uzzi,
The worst boss you've had,
Was a foul-mouthed emcee,
But he didn't shoot you,
He just wouldn't let you be.

So you don't know shit,
About their suffering there,
'Cause frankly, my dear,
I don't think you care,
You're too busy here,
Blowing hot air,
When you can't afford stuff,
You cry, "That's not fair!"

Just shut up and enjoy,
The life you have here,
'Cause things could be worse,
Than the worst things you fear,
On this side of the pond,
You can choose what you hear,
Elsewhere, hearing too much,
Gets you shot in the rear.

School the System

This is for those institutions that keep making money,
Off my education, an act that I don't find very funny,
Claiming to teach me, when all they do is waste my time,
I've learned more on my own, when I've not been confined,
To a tiny cubicle learning the same B.S. time and again,
I've even taught myself the Internet without you, my friend!

By investing in you, I wasted 15 years learning to be subservient,
And learning a system where I was but another numbered variant,
So I became a slave to its workings and planned procrastination,
If you don't agree, then they've already dumbed your imagination,
With their bells from Hell, which they also use in every prison,
And their restricted education, to make you fit in with their vision.

Now with that said, lets take you back to where this began,
Way back in 1819, when the Prussians laid out their plan,
A system created after Napoleon's rookie army had won,
At Jena, where some paid Prussian soldiers got outdone,
Starting in 1806, many worried another defeat may ensue,
So in 1819, the state began training soldiers to do as told to.

By forgetting their self-thinking, since it no longer mattered,
They'd unite the German states, which had all been scattered,
These "robotic" soldiers influenced many a visiting American,
Who in 1852, mandated "central schooling" yet again,
When brought to the state, it debuted in Massachusetts,
It then spread about like one giant, nonstop nuisance.

Until, as aforementioned, it was made mandatory,
In 1852, under federal law, it was to be made regulatory,
Ever since, we've lost nearly every childhood daytime hour,
And we've been taught how to live in fear of those in power,
These top dogs would exploit our fears and inexperience,
In essence, "kindergarten" detached us from our parents.

Fella to Fight

Hey there, big fella, how do you do?
I'mma knock your ass out, if what I'm hearing is true.
Did you really just walk your old ass into my place,
Just to start shit with my girlfriend, and throw food at her face?

Don't you know, man, that ain't how the shit work,
I be kickin' the ass of those actin' the jerk,
So look, man, you best be movin' on now,
'Fore I do you like Batman with ZERPLUNK and KAPOW!

Yep yep, motherfucker, I come ready to fight,
I'll shoot a jab at your face just to screw up your sight,
And if you still wanna come at me, talkin' your smack,
I'm a kick out your knees 'til your movement you lack.

So in case you don't follow, then let me repeat,
I'm sick of your yellin', man, bringin' such heat,
And if ever again we must run through this drill,
I'mma bust your mouth open, prob'ly fuck up your grill.

Step back, you dumb fuck, don't you make me react,
'Cause I'd waste you in seconds, this you know is a fact,
But still you wanna look hard, so you don't run away,
Fine then, you asshole, come on out and lets play.

Yep yep, motherfucker, I'm always willin' to fight,
And in fact, doing so, would probably bring me delight,
So man, here's a knife, please try to dish out some pain,
Never mind my laughter, as blood shoots from my vein.

You're swingin' for my jaw, but I'm duckin' out the way,
Then I'm comin' back hard, a roundhouse without delay,
And your ass is falling back, just the start of my attack,
Fifty punches to the skull, leave your face a bloody sack.

Still you're rising up again, guess you didn't get enough,
And you're lunging out at me, tryin' out some other stuff,
But I simply block it all, then I kick you in the balls,
Now you're grasping at your nuts, cryin' like Niagara Falls.

Yep yep, motherfucker, you came wantin' to fight,
But you picked the wrong asshole with whom to start shit tonight,
And in case, some day, you wanna settle the score,
I'll be ready and willin' to drop your ass to the floor.

U Were Wrong 4 Me

In some regard, I must admit,
You held some regard for me,
Then again, on the other hand,
You tried to be some fake O.G.,
And babe, since we're still friends,
I hope maybe you'll listen to me,
When I tell you that that's not you,
Stop trying to be what you can't be.

That's not to say, you weren't right,
And I'll say this here tonight,
'Cause I won't fret, it's the truth,
I thought we'd be naked in delight,
But then again, you knew that then,
It's not like I was hiding anything,
And like I said, that night in bed,
You weren't just some random fling.

You were cute, and oh so pervy,
But there was more to us than that,
We connected, we got each other,
You even drew for me my tat,
Offbeat humor, a love for music,
Mocking our own Latino-ness,
We both were smart, and oh so artsy,
So how'd we end without success?

But I don't want to be an asshole,
So tell me everything I screwed up,
Only this time, please come do so,
Where it may better this old schlup,
'Cause trust me, baby girl,
Nothing you could tell me nowaday,
Could leave me further scarred,
For I'm confounded, anyway.

See, I know how you think,
And I know just who you are,
You don't know how much I loathe,
Hearing folks speak from afar,
Guess I should've heard my sis,
When she came to me, and said,
That the girl I was seeing then,
Seemed a bit emo in the head.

But that was her, it wasn't me,
I think I bonded with your quirks,
They seemed like little challenges,
Built in to scare away life's jerks,
But now I feel like I'm that jerk,
And I don't even care if you know,
I feel like maybe you only said "yes,"
'Cause you couldn't tell me "no."

If you wanna date someone,
I hope you know that's cool,
Though I really hope this time,
You won't pick another fool,
'Cause with me, for instance,
I've been stabbed and shot,
But neither ever hurt as much,
As that Monday when we fought.

L'Ex

Well, ain't this some life?
Just when you've moved on,
Fate comes rushing back,
Like some satanic spawn.

Can staggering people,
Believe in their mind,
That their exes' success,
Ain't something they'll find?

Well, it hurts my soul,
That this, you believe,
With all of your talents,
How can't you achieve?

And though I was told,
That you'd do all right,
Now you're drunk-texting,
Midway through the night.

When first, you dumped me,
I didn't know what to do,
I've been through it before,
But never with you.

And though, it seemed,
That I'd never be healed,
Life gave me that lemon,
So I'd grow my own field.

Now, it hurts my heart,
That you feel like shit,
So lost in your sadness,
Your love, it has quit.

And though I was told,
That you'd be okay,
You're saying stuff now,
That you never should say.

See that man in my mirror,
Sure, he's quite a view,
But just a few months ago,
He had not a clue.

Then wandering aimless,
His path led to you,
I am what you made me,
Not the boy you once knew.

Hence, it hurts my head,
To see you this blue,
Any success I have known,
I'd know not without you.

And though I was told,
That you'd find your way,
I want you to know,
I'm just a phone call away.

So you've sat with the losers,
For about half a year,
That's only a fragment of life,
It ain't nothing to fear.

There's still plenty of time,
To follow your dove,
And to make of your life,
Something you'd be proud of.

This way, the two of us,
We can be like we said,
Happy for each other,
When one gets ahead.

Then, the next time we meet,
Despite your drunk breath,
We can be friends again,
Until we're taken by Death.

Crossfaced Crippler

Ever since I was a child,
I've watched wrestlers run wild,
On my T.V. set each week,
But now one's turned into a freak.

What Chris Benoit did recently,
Surprised all of those like me,
Since we knew him as the hun,
Who loved his family a ton.

Though he always seemed so great,
His recent antics make me hate,
What kind of coward binds his wife,
Then grabs his son to take his life?

Chris Benoit, you are an ass,
A useless bugger with no class,
And now I'm sorry I cheered you,
But whouldda guessed what you would do?

You are a coward and a punk,
Who left your fans in quite a funk,
How can we now go on to trust,
Someone else who we deem just?

And then there's Eddie, up in Heaven,
Whom you've known since y'all were seven,
And now his memory's tarnished some,
Since he befriended you, you bum!

You were the last one I'd have thunk,
Could be so cruel and full of junk,
But like a knife, you pierced my heart,
As you tore your world apart.

I've finally got air back in my lung,
And that's a first since you were hung,
But I'm proceeding cautiously,
Since you took with you a part of me.

Legal Basketcase

Down here there was a case,
Which questioned my belief,
How can I support the system,
When it stands behind a thief?

Here's the thing that happened,
A guy tried to rob a house,
And cut himself while breaking in,
Then sued the owner's spouse.

See, he'd cut himself on a glass,
That the lady'd left in the sink,
As he crawled through the window,
Which was on that kitchen's brink.

As if that weren't screwy enough,
The asshole judge sided with him,
He made the homeowners pay,
To heal this crook's wounded limb.

And then, some two months later,
A fat kid sued a fast food chain,
For giving him some man-boobs,
Is that not the epitome of insane?

But somehow, the fat kid won,
And so labels were applied,
On that company's fried food,
Common sense had been denied.

On yet another occasion,
Some kid flew off a swing,
While trying to be Superman,
And try that flying thing.

The shmuck fell on his face,
So he smashed it all to death,
This surprised the kid's mom,
Who must've been on meth.

So history again repeated,
Another lawsuit went awry,
And so that thing now reads,
"Swings won't make you fly."

What kind of legal bull is this,
That gives money to the dumb,
They're just lucky I'm no judge,
'Cause I'd so tell off the scum!

Tortured Chamber

There was a guy from Miami,
Who worked for a law firm,
And a San Francisco scholar,
Who'd come for just one term,
The two now worked together,
And they started secretly kissing,
So all did seem quite swell,
Until that day she went missing.

See, this guy was way perverted,
He always wanted to get busy,
So this one day, in particular,
Her machine launched his morning tizzy,
And soon he'd leave his house,
In relaxed-fit jeans that felt so great,
To drive over to her place,
Attempting just to fornicate.

But his lady was a tramp,
And she'd been sleeping all around,
This time was the first in which,
He'd seen her kneeling on the ground,
With her head bobbing repeatedly,
Off some other man's crotch,
And this other man was getting off,
While all he could do was watch.

"But was that the case?" he thought,
And then his emotions kicked in,
He could do more in this world,
Then just take it on the chin,
He could go concoct a plan,
To make everything seem right,
Which meant he'd get her back,
So he planned all through the night.

The next morning he called her up,
And she quickly answered his call,
Guess this time there wasn't anything,
Blocking those words stuck in her jaw,
So he asked her where she'd been,
When he'd called the night before,
She claimed she was out with friends,
Like some sleazy, lying whore!

He sucked on that misleading fact,
Until something in him snapped,
He said, "well, what'cha doing now?"
She said "nothing," she was trapped,
So he invited her ass over,
And she got there really quick,
He claimed he wanted just to please her,
Guess she thought of something thick.

But what he meant was something more,
Pleasure was just the lie he sold,
Knowing that it'd always work,
In getting the girls to his abode,
So when she came on over,
He poured her a drink laced with a pill,
Trusting him, she drank it down,
What happened next would make you shrill.

She awoke to find herself in cuffs,
Down in some secret basement,
Photos on the walls surrounding her,
Were of her previous debasement,
Right here's where she learned the truth,
And so she did let out a yelp,
When she learned he knew of her ways,
She tried to scream for help.

But there was a gag inside her mouth,
All her clothes had now been floored,
And razors hovered over her wrists,
As she was strapped to a hard board,
If she were to move an inch,
Hoisting strings would come undone,
And not only would she be naked then,
But she'd be in too much pain to run.

So he knew she was going nowhere,
Even though she thought she might,
He said "listen here, you dirty slut,
I'm only making your claims right,"
See, in his mind, a girl who lies,
Deserves her just desserts,
So he was going to beat her raw,
Until her whole dang body hurts.

This man stood over her limp body,
Carrying a barb-wired two-by-four,
He said he'd use it only if she lied,
Then asked, "Are you a whore?"
She shook her head from side to side,
Denying him the answer that he sought,
So those barbs cut deep into her flesh,
Leaving her bloodied and distraught.

He then asked her one more time,
"Are you or are you not a silly whore?"
She held her breath, claiming not,
And so he laid into her some more,
Then he decided to go another way,
And asked her this question instead,
"Did you sleep with a dude last night,
Knowing that's something I would dread?"

She nodded her head yes,
Which placed him in a spell,
So he cocked his arms again,
And his anger made him yell,
After three whacks with this stump,

There was a dent in this girl's skull,
And blood now stained her teeth,
As her eyelids grew so dull.

And though he didn't really care,
Her twitching body now did grieve,
So showing some compassion,
The man decided just to leave,
He dropped the bloodied wood,
To abandon that there place,
But still strapped to that board,
Freedom, she could not embrace.

So the next day at work,
People wondered where she was,
Why she hadn't quite called in,
Her whereabouts were all the buzz,
The gossip made this awful man,
Wonder, while in his leather chair,
Whether or not she had survived,
So after work, he went back there.

He found her body still strapped in,
Having bled until it died,
And since he'd been mistreated,
He laughed, instead of cried,
He thought justice had been served,
When really justice was nowhere,
And that poor girl "disappeared,"
Leaving her family in despair.

Sure she may have done some wrong,
But was it really deserving of all this,
I guess the moral of this story,
Is to just be careful whom you kiss,
And don't go trusting strangers,
Whom you don't even really know,
Since people can be so weird inside,
But keep it hidden down below.

Calinform Ya

Looking out my window through my one good eye,
Think I'll go surfing today under this clear blue sky,
'Cause I'm in L.A. for the first time in a while,
And riding some waves would really make me smile.

So I'm thinking of sleep, but I'm rising above,
And I'm putting on a suit made by Body Glove,
Think I'll let the Oakley's cover up my eyes,
So that the sun won't cause any bad surprise.

Outside, I've got my board about eight feet long,
Which I'll load into my woody like that Beach Boys song,
So get ready Malibu because soon I'll come,
And after surfing, I'll go home and drink some rum.

God, I love Cali 'cause, man, it's so laid back,
Unlike Miami where everyone's always on the attack,
This is the type of town that allows us to relax,
I love Miami, too, but seriously, such calmness it lacks.

No wonder many exes of mine moved out here,
To the land of the Raiders and this three-mile pier,
Where the movie stars of Hollywood look oh so hot,
And you might see them chillin' at your favorite spot.

Could you imagine you're chewing on a steak alone,
When suddenly, beside you, they sit Charlize Theron?
I can't speak for you, but I think she's a gorgeous star,
I'd choke on the meat, in hopes that she'd provide C.P.R.

See, in Miami, who would you do that with?
All we've got is Andy Garcia, Gloria Estefan and Will Smith.
And we can't go surfing either, for we haven't the waves,
We've got only the heat, to which we're nothing but slaves.

And that's why when I get some free time, I fly out here,
To where each hard body maintains a perfectly-tanned rear,
And where the bars are generous, serving two-dollar booze,
Where Rodney King has been replaced by gays in the news.

This town is quite progressive, which I like to see,
But it ain't too aggressive, which is just fine by me,
It's got the perfect mix of everything y'all would need,
From a unique music scene to a full bag of weed.

So tomorrow, I'll be heading back toward Miami,
But next time I come here, who is coming with me?
It's always more fun when you hit Disneyland,
With folks you like, doing stuff you've planned.

Here's to Your Wet Pants

Now roughly seven years ago,
A friend of mine turned the big two-oh,
And as a result, we flew to Nevada,
Rented ourselves a Nissan Armada,
Then hit the strip clubs and casinos,
And two of the more famous shows.

Though Siegfried and Roy acted gay,
And we caught a fight at Mandalay Bay,
Neither tigers nor boxing could compare,
Since the next day involved gang warfare,
Between Hell's Angels and every Mongol,
While we were chillin' at Harrah's Casino.

Without a clue of what this was about,
We hid the moment that fight broke out,
Tucked our asses under the poker table,
Alongside every person who was able,
And what we saw seemed quite unreal,
This fight right here was the real deal.

Overweight biker dudes risked their lives,
Amid ball peen hammers and Spyderco knives,
There may have been a crescent wrench, too,
The Mongols lost one, while the Angels lost two,
And one hundred twelve men in total were cuffed,
Until the cop cars all seemed so stuffed.

And you want to know the motive of this story,
The Hell's Angels appeared in Mongol territory,
Since they knew it as a quasi-Mongol headquarter,
And had read "California" on the gang's bottom roller,
They felt their vests were the only ones allowed,
To boast the state of which they were so proud.

But thankfully, with all the violence around,
No innocent gamblers died on that ground,
Since most everybody hid from the onset,
Allowing the rival gangs to settle their debt,
And still, we remember those birthday chants,
"Our dearest buddy, here's to your wet pants!"

True to Yourself

When all your words have been written,
Your thoughts pulled from their shelf,
What others think of you won't matter,
So long as you've loved yourself.

'Cause though your mom gave you life,
And your friends showed you a good time,
None of those folks linger behind you,
While you make your heavenly climb.

So what I want you to do,
When things start to worsen,
Is walk toward a mirror,
And have a chat with that person.

Make sure you two are okay,
For he's the one you must please,
And if you can't stand his face,
Then there're sins to appease.

So go and do what you must,
That way when your time comes,
Your soul can be at ease with itself,
And not have to sit with the bums.

Don't let other people dictate,
The things they think you should do,
Just always stay true to yourself,
And only listen to you.

For you can be king of the world,
And be known through the land,
But how much will that matter,
If God rejects your hand?

Musique

The music I listen to,
Makes me feel glad,
And if I were to lose it,
I'd probably get sad,
Whether it's Esthero,
The John Butler Trio,
My homie Fiona Apple,
Or Mr. E, the main Eel,
There's always someone,
Willing to make me smile,
With a catchy melody,
Unique lyrics and style.

Whether Ol' Blue Eyes,
Or the Man in Black,
Music never grows old,
And it never gets whack,
But if you do tire somehow,
Stray from the mainstream,
Let Zero 7 lead you to sleep,
Where Lamya can help you dream,
Or you can go another direction,
Maybe take a more Celtic route,
Flogging Molly can lay you down,
And the Pogues can put you out.

Either one you choose,
Will surely delight,
Nothing makes me happier,
Then a musical night,
From the Lords of Acid,
And the Squirrel Nut Zippers,
To them boys from the Faint,
When they sing of strippers,
I also admire Ani DiFranco,
Sublime's Bradley Knowles,
Fellow Cuban Celia Cruz,
And the notes of Billy Joel's.

Nothing sweats of romance,
Like sweet Marvin Gaye,
Nothing foams with anger,
The Black Sabbath way,
No one's made us dance,
Like Bob Marley's crew,
And no one's brought awareness,
Quite like the band U2,
There's really only one place,
Where you can right life's wrongs,
So we owe it to ourselves,
To listen to all of these songs.

Subconscious Tragedy

One day I woke to find,
My dream had come true,
I died during the night,
Courtesy of a bullet or two.

My family stood all around,
Shedding tears that seemed fake,
With hands full of blood,
And their mouths stuffed with cake.

And I floated away,
Now that my mission was done,
Straight to the gates,
Went this chosen one.

And I had a chat with St. Pete,
Told him how I died,
My mother done shot me,
With my sister beside.

Then he woke me up,
And I realized this scene was a fake,
So I reloaded my glock,
Since I've so much now at stake.

I went back to sleep,
Where again this shit came,
Someone with a weapon,
Dowsed me in a flame.

Seems every night,
Much like Wes Craven,
I have twisted dreams,
In which I face my raven.

How many people out there,
Are really gunning for me?
I need to escape,
This subconscious tragedy.

Not Too Late

I've just woken up and I noticed something different,
I gandered at the mirror, and saw a man that I'd envisioned,
As I laid in bed, years ago, listening to a story,
He was staring back at me, with a face so full of glory,
This was a face that now was housing many wrinkles,
On a path so enlightened, with a past that sometimes sprinkles,
This was a person who was very sure of where he was,
But who never forgot his roots, as he reminds those on his bus,
Folks like Sudoku man and the little kid with the toy truck,
Or little iPod missy, and the saxophonist hoping for a buck,
On this journey, they've all met, and each one said the same,
The man inside my mirror chases life and that's his game,
He calls it "carpe diem," because of how his story goes,
Always tries to seize the day, but that part everybody knows,
So the really interesting part, is the one that comes out next,
The way he makes life better is by making his complex.

All right, lets break, since that part needs some explaining,
See, for this man, the journey is the part that's entertaining,
He knows he's smart and can have it all, if he actually wanted it,
But he'd rather struggle, for he feels that makes things more legit,
So for instance, with his writing, sometimes he'll make it bad,
Just so folks will criticize, and he can note what makes them sad,
This way his final masterpiece will be the best he's ever done,
For those who once did raise their voice placed bullets in his gun,
And now the only shot that counts knows exactly where to shoot,
So his longing for a masterpiece is what keeps him so astute,
And the women all around him, always sending him some signal,
But this man realizes such love comes only 'cause they're single,
And the minute you take them out of that element, things change,
So instead of losing it, he'll just keep roaming 'round that grange,
Though he'll never find true love, you can bet he'll enjoy his ride,
Unlike the depressed husband who's now on his wife's bad side.

So if you get not what he's teaching, herein then he clarifies,
The meaning behind life isn't meant to be one that terrifies,
Life's meant to be a journey, not just some random destination,
The minute you stop hunting, that's like welcoming frustration,
If by twenty-something, you've already got a mortgage and a wife,
How will you find the time then to squeeze more out of your life?
So to all those people who've gone and quit our human race,
Come save those who haven't by telling them to slow their pace,
To bask in the world around them, for they only get one chance,
And at the rate life moves, we know not when's our last dance,
So instead of getting stuck at home, put on those nomad shoes,
And never stop chasing your dreams, for when you do you lose.
The man that's in this kid, for instance, is one who's satisfied,
For he has lived alone enough, to never once have had to hide,
And so he came to discover, that he's carved a wide-open path,
Which can now lead him anywhere, without some embedded wrath.

In Your Pursuit of Happiness

I seem happy 'cause I am,
It ain't no act, it ain't no sham,
But you want to know the why's,
So lets dissect through human eyes.

I mean, really, why be mad,
Happy moments trump the sad,
And no tears have ever turned,
Bad to good, nor good to bad.

Life is mostly our reaction,
When all the bad things happen;
You can sit there being crass,
Or you can get up off your ass.

You control your destiny,
Throughout all eternity;
Don't let anger weigh you down,
Just shrug and lose the frown.

'Cause what good would it do,
To let life's shit latch onto you?
Just go and get a clue,
Don't let your happiness undo.

Final Credits

Though I'm no Maya Angelou or Toni Morrison,
I still like to think I can hold my own with a pen,
So if you like the many poems, herein penned,
Please purchase the book and become my friend.

Now before I go, I'd like to spread some fame,
By thanking those who've made me, by name,
From my mom Marlene and my sister Michelle,
To journalism professors who put me through hell.

I'd now like to remember some folks who've died,
Like my grandma Siomara, who's still by my side,
And also Victor Bonachca, who was a great friend,
And my mentor Don Sneed, whose lessons transcend.

I'd also like to show love for a gal named Jill Bauer,
Who helped land me some jobs by using her power,
As did colleagues like Allan Richards and Deb O'Neill,
And Professor Reisner, whom we always called "Neil."

Thanks also to my two best friends, Gra-al and Bean,
For keeping life fresh when joining me on the scene,
To all of those people, there'd be no me without you,
And to all of you readers, for letting me do what I do.

Peace out, everybody!